Shepherd

Without Sheep

POEMS

C. J. STEVENS

JOHN WADE, Publisher

Published by John Wade, Publisher
P.O. Box 303
Phillips, Maine 04966

Library of Congress Control Number:
2001-135026

ISBN # 1-882425-14-6   (cloth)
ISBN # 1-882425-15-4   (paper)

Manufactured in the United States of America

FIRST EDITION

ACKNOWLEDGMENTS

I thank the editors of the following publications in which these poems and translations first appeared: *Accent* (England), *Ann Arbor Review*, *The Antigonish Review* (Canada), *Black Sun, Caliban* (England), *Camels Coming, The Cape Rock Quarterly, College Arts, Colorado State Review, El Corno Emplumado* (Mexico), *Cottonwood Review, Cyclic Magazine, Descant, Discourse, Exit* (England), *The Far Point* (Canada), *Florida Education, The Galley Sail Review, Grande Ronde Review, Illuminations, Invisible City, Jeopardy, Kansas Magazine, Kansas Quarterly, Maelstrom, The Miscellany, Modularist Review, New Frontiers, The New York Times, Nottingham Poetry Quarterly* (England), *The Old Red Kimono, Open Places, Other Voices, Podium, Poet Lore, Poetry Dial, Quill Magazine* (England), *Red Cedar Review, Resurgence* (England), *Riding West* (England), *South, South and West, South Dakota Review, Targets, Tombstone Nine* (England), *Trace, Tulsa Poetry Quarterly, Unicorn, The Villager, Voices International, The Washington and Jefferson Literary Quarterly,* and *Wisconsin Review.*

Further acknowledgments are made to the following publishers for permission to use translations in Parts II and III: *A. Manteau N.V., EM Querido's Uitgeverij N.V.,* and *Uitgeverij Heideland.*

BOOKS BY C. J. STEVENS

Poetry
Beginnings and Other Poems
Circling at the Chain's Length
Hang-Ups
Selected Poems
Shepherd Without Sheep

Biography
Lawrence at Tregerthen (D. H. Lawrence in Cornwall)
The Cornish Nightmare (D. H. Lawrence)
Storyteller: A Life of Erskine Caldwell

History and Adventure
The Next Bend in the River (Gold Mining in Maine)
Maine Mining Adventures
The Buried Treasures of Maine

Translations
Poems from Holland and Belgium

Animal Behavior
One Day With a Goat Herd

Fiction
The Folks From Greeley's Mill
Confessions: New and Selected Stories

CONTENTS

I Poems

RETURN OF A STRANGER

There was a time I knew my neighbors' habits
better than my own: no window shade or bolted door
could come between their lives and mine—we all lived
in one tight knot of human regularity.

And I could predict what would happen or would not:
people reacted with the mechanical accuracy
of clocks; they were unaware of the galloping seconds
as they rode on their luminous dials of likes and dislikes.

One of them, intricate part, fraction of the whole,
snug fit, I too could be looked into and through
as they watched me moving about behind crystal walls
or strolling up the strong lens of a sidewalk.

Now, a stranger among strangers, an outcast,
I return to the town of my childhood and stand
before the blinding walls of mortar and eyesores
of smudged glass with only my timeless fantasies
blossoming like wildflowers in the fields of my past.

THE DRUM

Whenever
the drum begins its beat,
and fifty men fall in;
become a hundred legs
of left and right: I'm more
myself than I admit.
There's something in my blood
that makes me want to march
with other men; to be
subservient to the drum.
Feeling the pulses hasten
and hearing the footsteps
across the heart—there's marching
in my blood. And I'm too ready
to move my legs left-right
when sounds get stuck on that
tight throat, when men march out,
and fifty legs are picked up
and dropped.

THE CLOTH MONKEY

The red-nosed monkey with the cloth head
and spongy thighs is sitting in one corner
of my son's crib. Tonight, the child will lay
my looks on the soft pillow, and sometime
before tomorrow comes, I'll smile at my son
and find my wife's expressions loose with sleep.
The little monkey will still be in his corner:
he'll look protectively at the child's chest
and stare with sawdust amazement at the lifting
and slumping. I'll look down and see nothing
surprising. I won't notice the little monkey
half-twisted beside the quilt; I won't remember
my most childish understandings. Later,
before I sleep, I'll wonder if my son
is covered. Tomorrow morning, the child will wake,
throw his little jungle mate from the crib,
and another night will be wrenched from my hands.

ZACK MARSTON

Ten soapy winters
scoured the town
before Zack Marston
drank himself to heaven.
Ten fat summers
dirtied themselves,
and ten lean falls
found comfort under
the bald elms.
Ten thirsty turns
around the sun
before the sexton opened
that paunch of earth.
Now, a sober breeze
goes up the walk—
we miss its whiskey breath.
The sexton limps
to the parched hill,
and heaven is a word
we mutter to ourselves
in that blameless wind.

SNOWSCAPES

1.
Shrugging myself
awake, I watched
the snow feather
the yard. The trees
were flapping their wings,
and a door sharpened
its yellow beak.
That was this morning.
Now it's afternoon
and the flock has left.
When the lively birds
gathered their feathers,
I thought of home.
Five thousand miles.
Thirty years. I've come
a long way to sit still.

2.

Into my thoughts
you come stumbling,
the panting tongue
of your shirttail
licking the brush,
and your shotgun
pointing down like
a crutch. And where
the hill limps off,
the bloodless track
of deer. I think
of your empty gun,
and the soft snow—
repentant as
always and hugging
your wet boots.

3.

Holding a log the way
I make love, I was dragging
white oak in the snow
over the hill to the saw-
horse. It was ten below.
I counted twelve sound hunks,
and each one on the block
was an uphill walk,
a kicked door, and the tumble
of sticks in the wood box.
Then back. A downhill slue.
And on my knees in snow
before the pile, I held
each log in the chill
as I would my own love.

4.

The log spins into the snow
and I can feel the wash of blood
boiling over a toe—I'm cut.
I slump to the ground, unlace my boot,
and slowly pull the sock from the wound.
A red flap of skin is perched
on the top of my big toe
like a cap. The raw footstep
of the ax will leave a trail of bruises
but I'm left whole—not badly hurt.
It takes an incident like this
for me to see how closely we live
at the blunt end or sharp edge of luck.

THE HERDSMAN

As a herdsman I would sit
late in my barnyard room
wanting sometime to tend
a herd of poems—to find
them waiting in the dusk,
far out where the pasture ends
and the woods begin, and sing
them back.

          But every morning
I would go back singing
to the cows; back to the smell
of dung and new milk.

Half pretending and half
believing someone would hear,
I kept singing. And I
would sing a little louder
up and down the tie-up
behind the steaming cows.

Even then I wanted
to be a good herdsman.

FOREFATHERS

They plowed the cornfields
with oxen and thrashed wheat
until their beards were golden

their fingernails were premises of grime
and from the caves of their pockets
came stray plugs of chewing tobacco

they wore sheepskin
and coarse woolen not
delicate linen and lace

they rode the hayfields
on horse rakes and wallowed
the swamps in search of foals

they were men who belched on lush greens
and draped their necks with soiled bandannas
and hauled manure in all kinds of weather:

these were the forefathers
poor New England farmers
they were well acquainted with dirt.

THE NOMAD

I'm more the nomad than the yeoman who
  kneels before the weeds,
and I've got arms and legs that should be
  used for raising crops.
I haven't got the herdsman's blood—
  it's only restlessness I've got.
It's this that makes me think I'm more a nomad
  at heart.
And aren't we all, not what our arms and legs
  predict?
Aren't we more beautiful than our faults:
flaws that lead us unknowingly to gifts?
What would my father's father say to this,
stooping in the last row of his corn?
God made me the shepherd I am without sheep.

AT SEA

I stood one night
on the top deck.
Behind me land,
and somewhere east
a land unknown.
Over the rise
into the next
uplifting wave
I gripped the rail.
I counted gulls,
saw the last light
of Newfoundland.
Then staggered down
the B-Deck stairs—
back to a room
of swaying steel.
Into the night
and a new life
beyond the last
sucked-under light
I felt the sea.

GOOD TIMES AND BAD

the house we built
was drafty and cold
the car broke down
the woodstove smoked
three times we hurt
ourselves that winter
our stars were unlucky
we felt trapped
then lethargy took over
in subzero weather
our house burned flat
everything we had
disappeared in flames
after the insurance
we went to europe
to live in the sun
then the acquisition
of property began
books-raincoats-hats
a savings plan for land
another gathering
of self-pity and doubt
all becoming
familiar as smoke
and we keep moving

LOST BALL

I found a ball.
It felt funny
in my soft hand.
(Nobody saw
the balding man
in the backyard.)
Holding a ball
is looking back.
Finding it is
nothing; holding
it is wanting;
wanting to live.
I ask myself:
you poor, poor fool,
just how many
are there to find?
And I can say
I don't care much.
One is enough
in my soft hand.

RESEMBLANCES

(For a cousin)

I can see a likeness
along the territory
of your lips: the smile
of an uncle when you
smirk, the raw-meat
lisp of a maiden aunt,
and our granny's brother's
cliff of dentures—teeth
so remarkably irregular
and steep. Even
the cleavers of your eyelids
remind me as we talk,
but I pasture politeness,
and you shyness, and slowly
the herd is numbered.
But we don't mention
resemblances. Only
names are inspected
like slabs of beef:
Crowell
Mearl
Ica
Helen
Earl.

I WAS LAUGHING

(Remembering Mel)

I was laughing
at some mistake
I made when the news
of your death came.
It wasn't the looking
down at my hand
attempting to relive
the violence; it was
the insane gift
wonder. It was this.
And closing my eyes
to the day, pretending
I died, I saw
only myself
with my eyes closed.
I didn't find
the yielding you
saw so clearly. Felt.

DOOLEY'S PLACE

Twisted around, the sky was upside down
and those big steamer clouds freighted the rain
under the pond. Blue Hill, submerged, had found
bottom. The world was all stretched out—"collapsing"
Dooley said. I got down, lowered my head
to the ground, lifted my legs: the birds were pumping
along, upside down. Then Dooley and I
were laughing. He laughed because the world was falling;
collapsing, he thought. I laughed because my head
hurt me. And because I didn't like the place.

CLIPPING

You remember
reading about
the man who was
blown to pieces
in the A-bomb
attack?—only
his shadow was
found. I sometimes
think of this when
I find myself
in a corner.

BEAR TRAP

Not to the beast
but to the bear in man
I speak.

          I share
an old uncertainty
that leaves me sly
with fear.

          There is
the bone reminder
that some animals
must snarl for love.

On hind legs
and heavy thighs
I rear—

          unyielding;
insensitive in the harsh air.

THE NEIGHBORHOOD

Someone is laughing
in the corner of my eye,
and faces straighten when I turn.
What someone said yesterday
is repeated today, and all I hear
must first be overheard. There is
no confrontation, only the slyness of words.
Voices are lowered and shoulders are bent.
(Dissection begins.) I come apart
between sentences—each piece
is placed where it can harm.
And yet this isn't always so:
when I get hurt or suffer losses,
neighbors put the pieces back
the only way they know. Concern
increases. I'm given
hands to shake and smiles to ape:
the old suspicions become a plotless story.
I am forgiven. My black and white
predicaments turn gray—
enemies are friends.

II Dutch translations

Ellen Warmond

SPEAKING

Speaking with the things
that know breath
but not language
one can call this spring

the houses and the foolhardy bridges
and the so-often-sorrowful cobblestones
the women with the swaying knees
the men with the self-assured hipbones

and the children who alternatively
imitate the one and the other
but who look more like kittens
always tripping over four paws
of serious endeavor

Ellen Warmond

LANDSCAPE

I strike your image from the rocks like water
rain I call you the gentle caressing
so arrogantly I unfold the landscape

mountains bend themselves over you
the wind folds all its wings around you
roads roll out their carpets at your feet
trees turn to look at you
my voice appeals to your echo in the valleys

in my blood grows inherently
the essence that meets you
and from your absence
arises your presence.

Ellen Warmond

IN SEARCH OF TIME LOST

1.
Only those who have shared your youth
know how the past tasted:
the new ready-to-wear skin
the undamaged lips
the sweet breath of bewilderment.

The code that we learned
from our impetuous beginning
we translate all our lives
but the old meaning eludes us.

2.
You taste just as you did of breath
of faded ritual turned into adventure:
now and later all love is self-love
we hold our lost youth in our arms.

Forget that you and I know this
only find us as we were.

Ellen Warmond

HERE AND NOW

Skin shuddering like a pond
under my breathless lips
I feed your blood with my blood
that is little but more than enough

I make you better I make
you better than you are
you make me human and more than human
you make me unprecedented

give us for now and later
for now and here
the singing power of water
the white light of pleasure.

Ellen Warmond

ONLY A QUESTION

With the once flowing body
obscured by the fear of viruses
with a mouthful of splintered bones
does anyone dare speak?
love
whispering
barely audible?

with the throat on the boiling point of a scream
the desperately evaporating blood
gurgling in the ears
does anyone dare hear?
love
smiling
barely visible?

Ellen Warmond

REPORT

An afternoon melts like snow
an evening falls as rain
here is the weather report for the evening
increasing warmth in the late night
a chance of heavy storms
warning for repugnance in the morning
here follows an extra report for people:
there is only one thing better than a person
another person

Ellen Warmond

ALMOST EVERYTHING, ALMOST NOTHING

Much is lost, almost everything
little is gained, almost nothing

except the getting used to despair
except the knowledge that it continues

and the reconciliation
with you in your mirror

Ellen Warmond

ROENTGENOLOGY

Dispute within the skin
between blood and intellect
to the last breath
in one's own hand

body
made lonely to the marrow
and transparent through emptiness

Ellen Warmond

UPTURNED PERSPECTIVE

Long before I knew you
my desire paced around you

I was desperate but we were together
now it is night
and we fit in our names

since you are here
I am alone again.

Bert Voeten

LISTENING IN THE MORNING

On the retina of the morning
I move weightlessly
with new arms and legs.

I am full of adam desire
the joy of breathing fills my chest
blushingly my ears hear
how my love walks into the day.

Doors wake up windows
the house becomes hypersensitive
the nerves of the rooms
pass her back to me.

Spies are the mirrors
that follow her from a distance
planks signal the step of
her unconcerned feet.

Pipes come to life
faucets sing and tiles
catch with enamel glimpses
all that I love.

Bert Voeten

JOURNEY

The day is a porter
he carries a trunk of sorrow for me
and a briefcase of light pleasures.

In the wagon wheel rut of the sun
I follow him
my heart full of weather reports
the umbrella of my soul
is tucked under my armpit.

I am traveling in my years
with two emergency rations of hope
but the door of the air blows shut
and the rain stands in front of it

now I can only
open my umbrella.

Bert Voeten

LITTLE SONG FOR OUTDOORS

Trot at full gallop, a horse in the sun
in the sunlight a plat du jour
on the green table of the meadow

trot far away from yourself—

death is a deep hole
and whoever falls in the well
must forfeit his turn.

Edithe de Clercq-Zubli

SONGS FOR AUTUMN INSTRUMENTS

I
escape
behind the reeds
where the birds scream
and escape
before the carrion of autumn.
the sun lies petrified
under the water:
a fossil of
drowned light,
a tender wound.

the age-old
throat sounds of
the slowly drinking
water.
a swamp sound
glides past
the skin of autumn.
the big red and
the big yellow blossoms
are ready to spring open.

II
your face is drowned
behind the tangible
behind
the mirror.

revolving doors
of autumn
turn wearily
in your dreamed eyes.

a small piece
of the evening turns
groaning in your body.

a dead sun
rose this morning
and later
drowned again.

Paul Rodenko

FEBRUARY SUN

Again the world opens like a girl's room
the street happenings sail out of white distances
workers build with aluminum hands
a windowless house of stairs and pianos.

The poplars throw with a kindergarten inclination
stuffed balls of bird voices
and very high an invisible airplane
paints light-blue flowers on light-blue silk.

The sun plays at my feet like a serious child.
I wear the downy mask of the first spring wind.

Hans Andreus

VIEW ON THE SEINE

The river of this city,
can always console me.
She has such soft arms and doesn't talk—
she only carries a smile of silk.

She can search far, become unreal.
With all her motion she is silent:
a reed bird, pollen, snow.
At night she is frighteningly calm,
and so she is dangerous.
Returning to the world she does not apologize:
again she accepts the embraces of bridges
who are her many lovers.

Marijke Fontugne

UNDER THE HIGH TREES, WAVING IN THE EVENING
the black river streams rapidly and with care.

When I lie on its banks
close to the earth
and I am dizzy from the waving of the branches
it seems to me that yesterday
I was a fish— a small gleaming fish—
and my real home
was the black river.

Under me beats the breast of the earth
as the leaves wave to the sky
and I let myself float
on the big constantly changing clouds.

Ankie Peypers

IN THE BIG ROUND LIGHT

In the big round light,
in the bowl of the morning,
move the previous days,
the previous deeds,
like small hurried fish.
They bump against the water plants
of sleep and night,
they bury angrily in the sand
from which in the morning one could
arise newborn, but for them.

Pierre Kemp

I HAVE TAUGHT HIM SOMETHING AGAIN

There I sit with my building blocks of flowers
singing, naming the blossoms
and the sun watches how I do it.

Sometimes her beams retouch what I do wrong
and I hear her stubbornly repeat:
I have taught him something again.

Pierre Kemp

SAD SONG

There I go with a dunce cap
full of stars on my head.
I once walked much straighter,
but then I still believed
that brides could come
and take the stars
for their veils. Those dreams
are now wasted.
Little has been left me
but this body without giving
and receiving, besides
my eyes can see no more brides.

Lizzy Sara May

SMALL BLUES FOR FOOTSTEPS

The night lights the city
the wind accompanies the street
the moon embraces the house
the bridge guards the water

I have no shadow anymore

the shore defends the water
the door secures the house
the silence harbors the street
sleep protects the city

I have no shadow anymore

M. Vasalis

HOMECOMING OF THE CHILDREN

Like big blossoms they come from the blue dark
under the freshness of the evening air
with which their hair and cheeks are lightly draped.
Caught by the strong grasp of their soft arms,
I see the full shadowless love
on the bottom of their deep-transparent eyes—
still unmixed with the human pity;
pity that comes later and has reasons and boundaries.

III Flemish translations

Jos Vandeloo

STONE MARSH

(winter)

Today I have been born
out of snow water and mist
in my breast
the cold poverty cries
of seagulls over parks
and sweet water

my scarecrow arms
stiff to the day

I want to see the sun
to step on my shadow
to rise above the lame houses
before the stone marsh
of the city petrifies me.

Jos Vandeloo

NARCOSIS

Must I count the miles
emptying before us
you in the sun
I in the rain

there are no royal engineers
to build between us
a new bridge

between our glass fingers
happiness like sand
a little water and sun
a little snow in the open hand

we are called human
and so are powerless.

Jos Vandeloo

CAVATINA

once you put
a goblin in my head
and you have wildly hunted
the elves in my heart

in this world
you are only
a maggot

and this infamous creature
with its lapping heart
I trusted too long

I will no longer live
like a sensitive seismograph
that faithfully virtuously
registers each of your tremors.

Jos Vandeloo

BEGINNING

From Lin Yutang
I have read words
raindrops of wisdom

I took off my hat
raindrops fell
summer rain on the beach
on my hot forehead

the rainword drops
ran into my mouth
and surprise mingled
with my spittle

then I understood
the wise words
of Lin Yutang.

Jos Vandeloo

DREAMS

searchlights
of my dreams
grope along stars
planets and moon

big mouths grin
at my dreaming
search for things
that don't exist

words without essence
are my dreams
stars where searchlights
never come

Jos Vandeloo

TELEPRINTER

Without faltering the teleprinter sings
with sinister regularity
its composition of an old melody
one of loving and possessing
of fantasy and mistaken identity
a wonder drug for rheumatism
and gray hair nostalgia
the teleprinter lays brick after brick
of the past to a skyscraper
and in the reeds of lowered eyelashes
now petrified to a tower of babel
there are still eyes like water
in which all dreams drown

Jos Vandeloo

POEM

Shining I shall inhabit you
my hands full of gifts
my fingers flowers
a hundred or a thousand candles
will festively
illuminate my body

we shall enter the night
under the gateway
of a transparent dream
until the morning like a hatchet
will fall from the sky
annihilating us.

Pol le Roy

ENTRANCE

The gods unlock
my deepest name
in the salvation of undaunted desire.

With the wings of the ibis
you nestle in the morning of my hands.
The grain becomes heavy
but already the light enters its dream.

The first scythes rustle.

Pol le Roy

POEM

The day your hand
discovers the black wind
and the roaring
around you—the sea
and its breakers

the hot-travelled ships
of bewilderment
the snow portals of silence
these are not exits either

so you stroll along a dead sea
alone with yourself
and that white dog.

Pol le Roy

POEM

Wall and steepness
blocks of silence too

women cut absent roses
stare at me with black stars
perfect beauty of forbidden fire

there is no way back
until the snow too
forgets itself in me

until I accept
death's point of view.

Pol le Roy

VOICES FROM CHAOS III

With full freedom in his smile
and on his hands all the distress
of which these self-abused lands suffered:
so he walked with measured steps to death—
as if the last prophet of this world
were leaving in the last morning-red.

He slipped into death as into a glove.

Then the guns shook in their madness.
And old hands picked at the feathers
that a torn-up bird leaves to memory.

The dead man lay like an unguarded morning-pasture
in the charmed attention of the mind.

Pol le Roy

RISE

Once where the tower stairs darken the stars
and only a glimmer parts me from my beginning
I enter the bottomless gate of liberation.

There is no world outside myself
my other self confesses against me
arch and keystone are my perfect vault.

Pol le Roy

CONFESSION

Together we loved life
we loved silence, the stars, and the late evening fires
together we loved those nights
we loved the winters, the fields of snow
together we loved those who had died
we loved our love, the hate, the sorrow, the shame
together we loved each other....

Leave me the dead song of our bound hands.

Pol le Roy

SPLIT WE ARE

Split we are
tragically speaking of what implacably
remains our truth and our hopelessness

silence star-turned silence
the forehead of the finale carries
the night smooth-stoned and hairy
tomorrow will appear without a mask

blind watchmen we are with petrified herds
tragically silent are the golden beetles
of the captured song

Paul Snoek

PARK POEM

In the pond of the day
I see old men with frankincense hair
and children in silent perambulators.

An arbitrary swan
wipes with a white sponge
all sound from the pond
and swims through the clouds.

A toy helicopter
strolls along paths of air
to the northern water south.

Paul Snoek

TOTEM

I wanted to be an emperor
in this life of dwarfs
but I could not forget
the softness of a peach.

I too have seen daily
the white throats of fear,
have feared the hard hands of light.
I could not forget
the full silence of the fishes
and remained an old child.

Now I have painted
my forehead with dream colors.
Day in day out I am your stranger.
I smoke a peace pipe.

Paul de Vree

in memory

obit 12-18-1946

you who proceed me in life, in death,
daily still I eat the bread
of your image, your thoughts,
each moment I can expect you,
there is no distance and locked grave.
in me you again accost things,
after each defeat the more experienced,
more patient, softer in your gestures,
and in a tender fight with hopelessness
you have gradually replaced the stress
from thirst to passion, from urge to deed.
I read it on your face as on mine,
until fear threatened each happiness,
until disgust blurs all sorrow,
until you arose again, truer partner,
the lips more broken, but in the words more sun.

Paul de Vree

BEHIND BARS OF UNSHED TEARS

behind bars of unshed tears
your wordless and heaped-plate image
with hands bread-fresh and feather-light
fingers that move like small caressing lizards
every movement declares that meeting is preservation
leaving the nest of the mouth a swallow dives away
over the quivering mirror of your cheeks
everyone returns to his polar night
after the greeting on the equator
with the gondola graphics of our cried-over boating

Gaston Burssens

PANORAMA

There are so many towers of broken humbleness
of which the gilded weathercocks carry no trace
There are so many streets sharply parting
streets that chase the loneliness to the eaves

They who teeter and creep along the gutters
and with the black cats sharpen their lamentations
on the stone of wisdom of a hidden owl

They know how each roof from peak to cornice
flattens the surface of their soullessness
how each tower of their recklessness
in which some scrawny bats live
would deny shelter to an owl that fed itself on mice

Gaston Burssens

BEWITCHMENT

The snow was never so white
nor so black my car
nor the throbbing of the motor so sonorous

So pale was never the hand of a mistress
nor so dark her hair
nor her voice so thin-textured as air

If now the snow lay like fur
over my cold shoulders
then the motor would not sing so softly

over the whiteness that is surely not white
not black like my car
nor like the voice of the mistress

Gaston Burssens

SELF-PORTRAIT OF THE READER

The landscape slides past us
a shabby cow on the side of the track
a white wall with the name of the village

The buttercups and daisies
stand in threadbare beauty beside the shabby cow
and have glided past our eyes and the dirty windows

We are the natives of this shy village
who despondently compare the mooing of the cow
with the tooting of the train whistle

Gaston Burssens

WRITE-OFF

Interrogations pose themselves as raw questions
with answers down to the rawest flesh.
We carry our fear personified
knowingly and unknowingly to the grave
with all the veneration and honor we owe ourselves.

All I can do for this drowning man
is have them fish me up like a worn-out shoe.

When I'm tired and drunk I do not care.
I was, they said, an insufferable bore.
It is the controversy between now and then.

IV Poems

TIME AND THE WINTER

Outdoors, the white, unmended patches blotch
the timber in the winter park. The curled
rock maples sift the snowflakes to their feet
where a fossil footprint with nowhere to go
resumes its promenade along the street
steps gently on the ice and disappears.

What if last autumn's curfew led a beast
to exile in his log or cave? The dawn
will thaw the frozen timepiece as the year's
iced gargoyles gag and pockmarked puddles strain
with witless laughter on the boulevard.

Time hangs like shirtsleeves in the stiffening weather.
Stilettos wait the victim where the drops
had synchronized a watch. Hours ago
—or centuries—an unidentified feather
replaced the bread crumbs in the slippery yard.

HOUSE VISIT

The house has being—almost as if you saw
its girlhood antics in a room of laughter;
heard the giggling timbers shift their secrets
within the bridal trueness of the walls;
as if you knew the green resilience kept
the pine boards dancing and made the lidded lintels
wink; as if you felt the attic's fever
yeasting with its nine-month loaf; saw
the plaster snap like a scolding matron's neck-
lace and found the dusty traces sprinkled
on the embroidery of doilies. Sometime,
somewhere in the kitchen, when you have stared
into the speechless expectancy of years,
a hag, who doesn't forget her girlhood giggles,
will creak toward you on the rot of her days,
her face dilapidated by the pleasures
of antic dreams rusting in the attic.

TRADE-OFF

In childhood
he was thought to be
sharp-witted but peculiar—"not
right in the head." He had
that strange mixture of
convention and unsettled
behavior to outlive: his mother's
conformity, his father's
wildness—both pulling
him down. He settled
for aloofness; an indifference
he never felt. It was this
that healed him, gave him
a life. Now, his own
children look at him with
strange eyes. He can't
tell them how much love
is hidden, nor does he want them
to crack open his disguise.

OLD SHOE

If he hadn't scuffed
my seams until
they popped, he'd still
be proud of my *Kiwi*
complexion and I'd be
licking his foot.
He wouldn't be
picking me up
by my laced hair—
he'd be caressing me
with a sock.
All I can
offer him now
is the hide of
a battered animal
and on my breath
the smell of
that last walk.

SNAKE STUDY

Ambushed in my coiled state among the weeds,
I sense the urgency of that long stick
above my head. This moving hugeness here,
that hunts relentlessly to shower hate
upon my funneled flesh, has come at last,
and I, compelled to stand my circled ground,
hiss my revenge, flick my pronged tongue in rage,
and brave the scream of sky upon my back.

The whirling last sensations in my eyes
will be the tumbled grass, the rush of air,
and I in blindness strike the nearer foe,
explode my weapons on some harmless trunk
of tree in suffocating haste, and die
a writhing line of velvet cut in half.

OLD SOW

Up to her knees in filth
she waits for her swill,
forelegs shaking the fence,
hind legs in the muck—
her appetite never varies.
The earth hardens
and someone sharpens a knife:
there is something mysterious,
even sensuous, hidden
in the paralysis of frost.
The sow rubs her back
on the pig-house wall,
and still squealing, she waits
for the snow. No one has
the courage to cut her throat.
All winter she scratches herself
on ice and the first warm days
find her gluttonous and her assassins
restless. But spring is no season
for pig killing, and the sow
with her litter knows this.

CHARACTER STUDY OF A TRAFFIC FATALITY

Delighted when her calisthenics wore the fat
from thighs and gave her buxom silhouette a show
of slender lines and loveliness—she was like that.

Pure girl and inspiration to the men who praised
the youth she had retained, defiant to the slow
revengeful years of blame, she told her mirror lies.

But sweet and soft cosmetic wonders left her dazed.
The coarseness in her life leered in her face,
and was unfortunate her friends agreed. She made
herself eccentric trying to create some trace
of serenity in her sad, declining world.

Her failure came one morning when at seventy-three,
intently flirting with her chances through the swirl
of traffic on the boulevard, one moment clear,
the next her last, she most reluctantly gave in
to the one thing she did and most completely fear.

THE WAITING

She's waiting for her mate
to reappear. The one
with white thighs and horns
cracked? Perhaps that one
or the lame Holstein
of two years back. Beside
the spruce gate she waits
with her legs spread wide.
She looks at the bars. She wants
to jump from the green lap
of grass onto the path
that circles to the barn.

CLOTHESLINE ESCAPEE

quickly his shadow
wraps around us
the torn rag
of a hand
flaps loose
a tooth flashes
like a hankie
as he begins
his starched laughter
two obsidian stickpins
jewel his vision
a smile wrinkles
his smudged lips
he's bleached
with information
then he waves
a laundered sleeve
it's time for him
to kick the breeze
like underwear
and leave

OLD ELM

Last night's
wind tore
an old
elm from
the ground.
The tree
fell and
Mr. Smith's
old shed
roof broke
the fall.
The old
elm now
leans like
the cane
that props
Mr. Smith.
One more
storm and
all will
be gone.

DOG SONG

Bury me deep
in an old wood's hole
leave me with roots
and bygone leaves.

Let the cold winds blow
let the branches bow
let next year's frost
and next year's snow
cover me over.

Let the dry rot crawl
let the long grass sleep
let next year's leaves
and next year's sleet
go prowling over
an old wood's hole.

TOM

Nelson Demlen
wanted fame.
Have you ever
heard of him?

And poor Bill Bing
loved life.
His monument
is a mountain.

Amos Cooley
had everything
but his young wife.

Cooley, Demlen,
Bing—Tom's old friends.

Tom survives them.
And he, he wants
nothing.

RAW MATERIALS

"Who needs the raw materials of life?"
he asks while they are sitting in the stuffed chairs.
"Who needs these things?" His wife
looks up and smiles at him. (A pinup
suns herself on a white page.) He folds
the magazine; slaps his knee. "Who needs
these things?" he agonizes to the clock.
The twelve-eyed wench stares back with bedtime eyes.
His wife doubles her yarn and yawns.
It is time to go upstairs and stare at the dark,
he thinks. Time to face these things.

THE CHILD

The child
stood by
the rail-
road tracks.

She had
a sad
sad smile.
Bare feet.

There by
the tracks
she watched
the train.

The child
waved back
in the
light rain.

THE HIRED GIRL

In the early nineteen forties
trying desperately to see
Betty Grable in the scratched
world of our kitchen mirror, you
truly succeeded with your grain-
bag dresses and monotonous shawls.

Such loveliness now would be meaningless.
Who can experience illusion
and make it come true in a mirror
and walk beautifully to bed?

Well you did, after the dishes
were stacked away in the back pantry,
the cat let out, and the floor scrubbed
on your knees in supplication
to the incredible nineteen forties.

POSSESSIONS

He's stuck in the middle of life
with more possessions than he'll ever use:
ten acres of brush on a dying farm,
two dry goats, and fifty roosters he can't kill.
He's got a cultivator in a tumbledown barn,
a three-legged antique milking stool,
an old rocking chair with a split arm,
an assortment of water pipes and rusty wrenches,
a ten-foot ladder with weak rungs—this inventory
could go on forever. And probably will.
The things around him drive his piled-high mind
to find space for the next day's dream.
His life is becoming a janitor's nightmare.
"An endless warehouse is urgently wanted"—
this should be his ad in tomorrow's newspaper.
Instead, he'll lean his three ironing boards
against the attic wall, dismantle the bedsteads,
tighten the coils of surplus haywire,
separate his collection of gaskets and screwdrivers,
and he'll be one day older.

About the Author

C. J. Stevens is a native of Maine. His poems, stories, articles, Dutch and Flemish translations, and interviews have appeared in approximately five hundred publications worldwide and more than sixty anthologies and textbooks. He has taught at writers' conferences and seminars and has lectured widely. His books include poetry, biography, fiction, translations, history and adventure, and animal behavior. Stevens has traveled extensively and has resided in England, Ireland, Holland, Malta, and Portugal.

DATE DUE

MAY 1 1 2006			

Demco, Inc. 38-293